The New York Times

POCKET
MBA
SERIES

ORGANIZING A COMPANY

25 KEYS TO CHOOSING A BUSINESS STRUCTURE

S. JAY SKLAR, J.D.
JOSEPH N. BONGIOVANNI, J.D.
Fox School of Business and Management
Temple University

Lebhar-Friedman Books
NEW YORK • CHICAGO • LOS ANGELES • LONDON • PARIS • TOKYO

For *The New York Times*
Mike Levitas, Editorial Director, Book Development
Tom Redburn, General Series Editor
Brent Bowers, Series Editor
James Schembari, Series Editor

Lebhar-Friedman Books
425 Park Avenue
New York, NY 10022

Copyright © 2000 *The New York Times*

All rights reserved. No part of this work covered by the copyright
hereon may be reproduced or used in any form or by any means—
graphic, electronic, or mechanical, including photocopying,
recording, taping, or information storage and retrieval systems—
without the written permission of the publisher.

Published by Lebhar-Friedman Books
Lebhar-Friedman Books is a company of Lebhar-Friedman Inc.

Printed in the United States of America

Library of Congress Cataloging-in-Publication Data
Bongiovanni, Joseph N.
    Organizing a company : 25 keys to choosing a business
structure / Joseph N. Bongiovanni, S. Jay Sklar.
    p. cm.—(The New York Times pocket MBA series ; vol. 5)
    Includes index.
    ISBN 0-86730-772-2 (paperback)
    1. New business enterprises. I. Sklar, S. Jay. II. Title   III. Series.
HD62.5 .B568   1999
658.1'1—dc21   99-27691
                                                         CIP

DESIGN & PRODUCTION BY MILLER WILLIAMS DESIGN ASSOCIATES

Visit our Web site at lfbooks.com

Volume Discounts

This book makes a great human resources training reference.
Call (212) 756-5240 for information on volume discounts.

INTRODUCTION

LEBHAR-FRIEDMAN BOOKS is proud to present *The New York Times* Pocket MBA Series, 12 invaluable reference volumes that are easily accessible to all businesspersons, from first level managers to the executive suite. The books are written by Ph.D.s who teach in the MBA programs in some of the finest schools in the country. A team of business editors from *The New York Times*— Mike Levitas, Tom Redburn, Brent Bowers, and James Schembari—provided their own expertise to edit a reference series that is beyond compare.

The New York Times Pocket MBA Series offers quick-reference key points learned in top MBA programs. The 25-key structure of each volume presents an unparalleled synopsis of crucial principles of specific areas of business expertise. The unique approach to this series packages academic books for consumers in an easy-to-use trade format that is ideal for the individual businessperson as well as an excellent training reference manual. Be sure to get all 12 titles in the series to complete your own MBA education.

Joseph Mills
Senior Managing Editor
Lebhar-Friedman Books

25 KEYS TO CHOOSING A BUSINESS STRUCTURE

CONTENTS

KEY 1

How to begin: choice of business organization

The first decision an entrepreneur has to make before engaging in a business activity is the choice of a legally recognized business organization form. This can range from a sole proprietorship to a general partnership to statutory hybrids such as limited partnerships, limited liability partnerships, limited liability companies and to various statutory corporate formats. This chapter will discuss the basic attributes of each entity. No single form is "better" than any other. But the entrepreneur should review the differences in each format—in legal liability, tax treatment and organizational structure—and choose the one that makes the most sense for her business.

A sole proprietor has unlimited legal liability for all business obligations, and this liability extends not only to the business's assets but to his personal assets. The proprietor also has sole management authority, and all his business income is taxed as his personal income.

A sole proprietorship lasts as long as the proprietor wants. It can be transferred to another person, but is otherwise dissolved upon his death.

A general partnership is, in its simplest form, a sole proprietorship of two or more persons. The partnership is created by the agreement of the parties. While a written agreement is not required, it is highly advisable to avoid dissension when one of the partners dies or wants to leave, or when other problems arise. You should ask a lawyer to help draw this up, especially as she can talk freely about sensitive issues that you might not bring up yourself, such as termination procedures, a formula for the distribution of assets and the use of the partnership name.

Each partner has unlimited liability for all business obligations, and this liability extends not only to partnership assets but to the partners' personal assets. This exposure means, obviously, that great care should be exercised in the selection of partners.

A partner can assign his interest to another but that person does not have full rights as a partner.

All partners have the right to participate in the management of the business and receive their share of partnership income. And each partner is taxed individually on his share of partnership income, whether the income is received or not.

A limited partnership is created by agreement of the parties and compliance with the relevant state statute. It consists of at least one general partner and one or more limited partners. The general partner has unlimited liability for all business obligations.

The liability of each limited partner is "limited" to the amount of capital she has contributed to the business. She can lose her liability protection, however, if she participates in management but fails to indicate to people with whom the partnership does business that she is a limited partner.

Limited partnerships are usually formed to give investors in such ventures as real estate and equipment leasing tax advantages that aren't available elsewhere. Generally, the limited partner's goal is not to be part of management, but rather to make money and keep more than if the business were conducted in a corporate form.

A limited liability partnership is created by agreement of the parties and compliance with the relevant state statute. The key distinction between this type of partnership and the general or limited partnership lies in the liability of the individual partners for business obligations. As this type of partnership entity is of recent vintage, the states differ in how they treat a partner for acts committed by other partners. As more fully discussed later, some states hold partners liable only for their own acts, others for the acts of subordinates as well.

A family limited liability partnership is much like the limited liability partnership except that the partners must be related as defined by the state law.

A corporation, often called a "C" corporation, has as its central legal characteristic the limited liability of the shareholders for business obligations. The only risk a shareholder faces is the loss of the capital invested in the business. While this limited liability can be offered to certain investors in some of the statutory partnership entities, unlike them, a

> Did you ever expect a corporation to have a conscience when it has no soul to be damned and no body to be kicked?

Lord Chancellor Edward Thurlow

corporation also offers an easy transfer of the shareholder's stake to outside investors or to heirs. Corporations which are also created by compliance with the relevant state statute have other attributes discussed elsewhere in this book that make them desirable to entrepreneurs.

A close corporation is either specifically formed as such or is a converted "C" corporation. The major difference is that while a "C" corporation must be governed by a board of directors, the shareholders of a close corporation can adopt a by-law permitting it to be governed directly by the shareholders.

This eliminates a great deal of corporate paper-work, but will usually work only if there are few shareholders who share the same corporate vision.

Certain restrictions apply to close corporations that scare off some investors. They cannot go public, and they have the right to limit the number of shareholders and curb the transfer of shares, for example.

A professional corporation, also created by compliance with state statute, can be established by people in certain professions requiring a state license, such as law, medicine, accountancy and architecture. It can not engage in any business other than the specific professional services of its shareholders, all of whom must be licensed in the profession. The impetus for formation usually revolves around questions of taxation, pension benefits and other employee benefits generally not available in a general partnership. The liability of shareholders for corporate obligations varies from state to state.

A real-estate investment trust is a corporate entity created for the purpose of investing its capital in real estate ventures. The income earned is subject to various restrictions as to its distribution and the portion of income that must be paid out to share-holders.

A limited liability company is a cross between a general partnership and a limited partnership. An L.L.C. owner's liability for business obligations is limited to the capital he has invested, and profits are taxed as they would be in a general partnership. An L.L.C. can vest management authority in its member-owners or in outside professional managers.

A 1997 change in Internal Revenue Service regulations simplified the process by which an L.L.C. can gain the benefit of being taxed for Federal tax purposes as a general partnership. Prior to 1997, the I.R.S. had a so-called "four factor" test, which made an L.L.C. liable for separate entity taxes if it possessed two or more of the following characteristics: limited liability, continuity of life, free transferability of interest and centralization of management. While this "test" has not been abolished, the I.R.S. has adopted regulations permitting a non-corporate entity to elect the manner in which it wants to be taxed, as partnership or a corporate entity.

Care should be taken however, as some states still treat an L.L.C. as a separate tax entity notwithstanding their federal tax status.

KEY 2

Getting started

To create a business entity, you'll have to choose a name, pay certain costs and keep certain records. Here's the rundown:

PICKING A NAME

If a sole proprietorship or partnership uses a name other than that of the owner or one of the owners, it must register a so-called fictitious name (for a fee, of course) and advertise it in a local paper. First, though, you should make sure the proposed name isn't identical or similar to an already registered fictitious or corporate name. Most states won't notify filers of a possible conflict, as they will in the case of a corporate name.

A limited partnership includes its name—usually followed by the designation "L.P."—in its original filing with the state. Be careful about using the name of a partner, though; some states ban the practice and others might revoke that partner's limited-liability protection.

In general, whatever the corporate entity, the name must not be identical or similar to an existing company's, must not mislead the public as to the nature of the entity's business and must not use the term "bank," "insurance company" or "trust company" unless that's what it is. Some jurisdictions require the name to be related to the nature of the business conducted and to include a denominator or its abbreviation, for example "Corporation" or "Corp."

PAYING THE COSTS

There are no state-mandated organizational costs for a sole proprietorship or general partnership, aside from the filing fees and advertising for registering the fictitious name.

Other partnerships and corporate entities generally must pay a state filing fee and often must pay for legal advertising. Most states require corporations to buy a corporate kit, containing by-laws, minute books and share certificates. And some owners will also end up paying to reserve a name for their business or to conduct a search of available names. But the total of all these costs is usually under $1,000.

Filing services will do the paperwork for about $125, or more if you are in a big hurry. And of course, fees by lawyers, accountants and other professionals for such services as preparing by-laws, writing buy-sell agreements can thin your wallet.

Limited partnerships must file certain information with the state, usually including the entity's name and registered location and each partner's name and business address.

For the various forms of corporate entities, articles

of incorporation must be filed, setting forth the corporation's name, registered office, capital-stock structure and term of existence, as well as the name and address of each incorporator. Sometimes, other information is also required, like the nature of the corporate business, the powers of the shareholders and the identities of the officers or directors. Note: The drafter of the articles should be careful not to encumber the articles with provisions that could hinder future corporate activity. Such provisions can be eliminated only by filing an amendment of the articles.

Records to keep

Statutory record-keeping requirements for a sole proprietorship and general partnership are minimal. All businesses should keep accurate accounts of income and expenses and copies of all business correspondence. A partnership is required to keep its partnership books at its principal place of business or at an agreed upon location. The various limited partnership entities are required to maintain at their registered office a list of partners names and addresses, copy the certificate of partnership issued by the state, partnership tax returns and copies of the current written partnership agreement and financial statements for the past three years.

Corporate entities are usually required to maintain at the corporate registered office, books and records of account, minutes of the incorporator, shareholder and director meetings, the by-laws, corporate resolutions and the names and addresses of shareholders and the number of shares they own. It is advisable to also maintain a current copy of any buy-sell agreement and employee contracts.

Whatever the form of your corporate organization, be sure to follow the letter of the state's filing requirements; failure to do so could jeopardize your liability protections.

Even if you haven't formed a legal entity, be careful what you say in your business dealings. The courts have ruled that if you talk or act as though you are a partner, you have in effect created a partnership "by implication"—and you can be held legally liable for you words and actions as though you really were a partner! And the standard the courts will invoke is not what you think you said or did but what a third party believed you said or did.

Can professionals like lawyers or physicians share office space and expenses without being regarded as partners? Happily, yes. But don't attach your names to the same signs or stationary, unless the sign or letterhead makes it abundantly clear that you are not parners.

KEY 3

Personal liability exposure for sole proprietors

The sole proprietor has unlimited personal liability exposure for all obligations incurred in the operation of the business, including contract obligations, debts and torts. This responsibility covers not only the actions of the proprietor but also the actions of employees, agents acting on behalf of the proprietor and possibly even independent contractors working for him. This liability exposure compels the proprietor to exercise the highest degree of care in hiring employees and in establishing an appropriate course of conduct for all those acting on behalf of the business. It's possible to buy insurance to reduce this risk, but it can be expensive.

The sole proprietor is personally responsible for the payment of all his business's taxes, including state and federal income and payroll taxes and the state sales tax, if any, and risks serious penalties, including going to jail, for failure to do so. Likewise, the sole proprietor can be held accountable for any violation by his business of state and federal law, including environmental, anti-discrimination or corrupt practices statutes.

This unlimited liability is onerous not only because of the potential harm to the business itself and its reputation, but also because the business owners personal assets—her house, bank accounts and other property—can be seized to pay the business's debt and other bills, including liability judgments.

Some limitation on property exposure might be available in those jurisdictions that give added protection to property owned with a spouse. But property that is jointly held with someone other than a spouse can be seized by a creditor of the business to the extent of the proprietor's interest in the property.

Lending institutions will ordinarily not lend money to a business owned by an individual unless that person's spouse signs the loan agreement. This would expose jointly held property to seizure for the business's debts. That's not a bad as it sounds. After all, with a larger pool of assets to go after, the lender will be more generous. Besides, banks are also unlikely to make a significant loan to a corporation that is new or has a small capitalization unless the owners, and perhaps their spouses, guarantee the debt.

Okay—we've painted a pretty grim picture of the liability risks in opting for a sole proprietorship, Why on earth then would anybody choose this form of business organization ? Well, hundreds of thousands of people have, and for good reason; it gives them exclusive control over their business. Besides, a judicious use of insurance and spousal joint ownership can lessen the financial risk, especially where the likelihood of litigation is low.

KEY 4

Personal liability exposure for partners

The partners in a general partnership not only assume personal liability for their own actions and those of employees and agents (as does a sole proprietor), but also for the acts of the other general partners. This shared responsibility can result in the exposure of all of the partners' personal assets to seizure and sale.

This exposure exists even for behavior that is not permitted by the partnership agreement. The breach by a partner of his obligations under the partnership agreement can be the basis of a legal action by the other partners for damage done not only to partnership assets but the assets of each partner. However, any recovery from the erring partner made in this way will not provide immediate relief from the action of the outside party who has filed a claim against the partnership.

Just as a sole proprietor has to exercise judgment and discretion in the selection of employees and others acting on behalf of the business, an entrepreneur must be careful in the selection of her partners. There is a tendency to only look at the positive aspects of joining forces with another person to make a profit. That's a mistake; the background, experience and assets of any potential partner should all be carefully evaluated. So should his personality and life style; the fact that a potential partner gambles heavily or has been divorced three times could be a harbinger of future problems. Selecting a partner is akin to selecting a marriage partner. Look before you leap.

A partner's liability is not limited to the proportional share of the capital that she has contributed to the enterprise. If one partner contributed 90 percent of the capital and the other 10 percent, and if the 10 percent partner incurs an obligation on behalf of the partnership, all the partnership assets can be utilized to pay this obligation. Furthermore, if the partnership assets are insufficient to satisfy the creditor, the majority partner's personal assets can be seized. In some states, the creditors of the partnership must first satisfy a judgment against partnership assets before proceeding against the non-partnership assets of the individual partners. Other states will permit the creditor to execute the judgment against the partners as a group and individually, or "jointly and severally" in legal parlance.

What this all means is that partners have what lawyers call a fiduciary relationship, a commitment based on utmost trust and loyalty to one another and to the goals of the partnership. A partner would violate this duty if she acted for her own benefit and not for the benefit of the business. In order to see if a partner has acted as she should, you have to look to the written partnership agreement, if there is one. (As we'll point out later, while there is no legal requirement for a written partnership agreement, not having one is very foolish.)

Many parterships limit the actions of individual partners, stipulating, for example, that any purchase above a certain amount must be approved by a majority of the partners. If a partner oversteps his authority, however, his decision is nevertheless legally binding unless it can be demonstrated that the other party to the contract was aware or should have been aware that the the partner was violating the agreement.

However, the other party does have some responsibility to show due diligence. What you have to consider is: Would an outsider reasonably believe that the partner has authority to bind the partnership? No one blows a whistle and says, "Authorized partnership action!" or "Unauthorized action!" This puts responsibility on anyone dealing with a partnership to make sure one partner has the authority to act on behalf of the partnership, particularly if a lot of money is involved.

All partners must realize that any partner has not only the authority as set forth in the partnership agreement but the apparent authority to act on behalf of the partnership and each partner. This means any partner can take actions not precluded by the partnership that are necessary to carry on the daily, ordinary operations of he business. No partnership agreement can set forth every act that a partner can or can not do.

There is a limitation on the personal liability of a newly admitted partner. The Uniform Partnership Act—the law in a majority of the states—provides that only partnership assets can be used to satisfy the new partners' obligations for debts incurred before she became a partner. There is no personal liability on the new partner but their capital contribution can be use to satisfy these prior incurred debts. This protection can be limited or waived by the terms of the Partnership Agreement.

KEY 5

Personal liability exposure in a limited partnership, a limited liability partnership, or a family limited liability partnership

A limited partner in a properly formed limited partnership assumes less liability than she would in a general partnership or as a general partner in a limited partnership.

Before providing any capital contribution to a limited partnership, an investor must assure himself that the limited partnership was properly formed in accordance with state law. As noted previously, a written agreement is generally not required to form a general partnership. It is also possible for individuals to be considered partners in a general partnership even if that was not their intention. We discuss this more fully elsewhere; suffice it to mention here that if individuals create in others a reasonable belief that there is partnership, a general partnership can be deemed to exist. This can not happen in a limited partnership because a limited partnership can only exist if the documents required by state law are filed.

A limited partnership can be organized with a

corporation as the general partner and the share-holders of the corporation as the limited partners. This structure reduces these individuals' liability exposure. Alternatively, you can have a limited partnership in which one of the limited partners is also the general partner.

If a limited partnership fails to follow the requirements of the state law that governs its operations, most states would contend that a general partnership has been created and would hold all those who contributed capital to the venture liable for partnership obligations to the same extent as the general partner in a general partnership. If a limited partner becomes aware of a failure to completely comply with the statute, he can avoid liability by filing an amendment to the original filing or by renouncing an interest in the profits of the partnership.

Having insured herself of the proper formation of the limited partnership, the investor will have liability for business obligations only to the extent of capital contributed. This is similar to the liability of a corporate shareholder for corporate obligations. The general statutory restriction on a limited partner is the right to participate in management. Even if the limited partner participates in management, there will be liability only if a third party has reason to believe the limited partner is a general partner. A limited partner should take great care when acting on behalf of the limited partnership to clearly indicate he is a limited partner and not a general partner.

An investor should review the certificate of limited partnership—the document issued by the state to certify that the limited partnership has been formed according to state law—so as to fully understand his financial obligations. In some instances, the certificate of limited partnership will provide for the contributions of a limited partner to be made in installments over a number of years. These contributions may be a set amount or may increase or decrease over the time period involved. If a limited partner fails to make these payments, creditors can make a direct claim against him for the money he owes. This is similar to the treatment of a stock subscription by investors in a corporate entity. Any such additional capital contribution obviously put more of the limited partner's funds at risk.

Limited liability partnerships are a recent development and are used by professionals who normally do business as partnerships, such as lawyers or certified public accountants. They are created by compliance with the appropriate state statute, much as a limited partnership is. The impetus for forming such an entity is that it allows the partnership to continue as an entity for tax purposes but limits the liability of the partners. A partner still has liability for torts she herself commits. The extent of this personal liability limit varies from state to state. However, under the law of Delaware an innocent partner is protected from the "debts and obligations of the partnership arising from negligence, wrongful acts or misconduct." Other states use terms such as obligations arising from "errors, omissions, negligence, incompetence, or malfeasance." Most jurisdictions require professionals who form an L.L.P. to obtain a statutory minimum level of malpractice insurance.

Partnerships like accounting or law firms that have many members or have offices in several states find this type of entity desirable, particularly in those states where the liability of partners other than the erring partner is limited to those in a close supervisory capacity to the errant partner. In an accounting firm, if a partner in a West Coast office commits negligence, only that partner and those who immediately supervised him will be liable. A partner in an East Coast office with no connection to the activity in question would not risk personal liability. This arrangement clearly would not work well for a small partnership in a single location because it would be difficult for a partner to claim no supervisory or other connection with the activity in question.

As these entities are relatively new there are still a number of questions about the extent of this limited liability in states outside the state in which the limited liability partnership was formed. If it is envisioned that the L.L.P. will do business in another state, it is imperative that a determination as to how that state limits personal liability be ascertained. You can not assume that your home state liability protection will be honored in the other state. Furthermore, the supervising partner of the errant partner in most states will also be held liable for the actions of the errant partner. Another question is how to apportion liability if more than one member of an L.L.P. is negligent. Are all partners liable, as in a general partnership? Or is there proportionate liability, as some states have declared to be the case?

An interesting variation on L.L.P. is the F.L.L.P., family limited liability partnership, in which a majority of the partners are related to one another as spouses, children, grandparents, parents, siblings, nieces, nephews and cousins. All partners must be people. A person acting in a fiduciary capacity to another can also be a partner. A F.L.L.P. can be useful as an estate planning method for many family owned entities, including family farms, because a discounted value can be placed on the business, lessening future estate tax obligations.

I never got very far until I stopped imagining I had to do everything myself.

Frank W. Woolworth

KEY 6

Personal liability exposure for owners of a corporation

A shareholder in a properly formed corporate entity does not expose his non-corporate assets to liability for corporate obligations arising out of business debts, torts, contract obligations or actions of employees and independent contractors. The only risk is the loss of the value of the investment. This protection of non-corporate assets makes the corporate form desirable for many entrepreneurs.

However, a close review of the nature of the business and of the extent of personal assets, as balanced against the time and expense of forming a corporate entity, may result in a decision to forego the liability protection. First of all, corporations are required to keep more records and are more costly to maintain than other forms of business organization. Moreover, limited liability doesn't have much practical meaning for the owners of many startups. They will always be liable for their actions and while they won't have direct personal responsibility to repay their business debts, lenders are likely to insist on personal guarantees for repayment from them anyway.

Add to that this fact: Shareholders must always refrain from any conduct that would cause a court to ignore the corporate structure and hold them liable for corporate obligations. That is to say, if personal and corporate actions are commingled to such a degree that it becomes difficult to determine if the action was for the benefit of the corporation or the individual shareholder, loss of the immunity from liability can result.

For example, if a shareholder pays her personal bills from the corporate accounts or corporate bills from her personal account, if she takes money from the corporate account without the formalities of making sure the withdrawal is treated as salary, or if she makes personal use of corporate property, she is asking for trouble. By the same token, a shareholder who owns several corporations must avoid juggling their accounts or making any questionable financial transactions like issuing shares for less than fair value or paying dividends if the corporation is not in a healthy financial position. The beneficiaries of such behavior can be held liable and forced to return the funds or repay to the corporation the fair value of shares received.

Further personal liability could result if a shareholder or potential shareholder has failed to fulfill her obligations pursuant to a stock subscription agreement to provide funds in return for shares in a to-be organized corporation.

Shareholders in small companies in particular must be sure to follow the corporate formalities in operating the business.

The incorporation process must be completed, directors appointed, officers selected and by-laws adopted once the certificate of incorporation is received from the state corporation bureau. All this can be done by the attorney who handled the incorporation process. Other required actions would be the opening of a corporate checking account, obtaining necessary business licenses in the corporate name, writing resolutions for corporate actions and holding corporation meetings that are required by state or federal law. None of these responsibilities are particularly onerous, but they must all be done.

Mind you, as long as the corporation meets its obligations, none of the above will matter. It is usually only after the corporation gets into severe financial trouble that creditors start to look around for a way to hold the shareholders liable.

If a shareholder is also a corporate officer or director, she must be careful to make sure the corporation follows all applicable statutory requirements. If the corporation is found to have violated a statutory obligation, penalties can be assessed against the corporation as well as officers and directors for failure to exercise proper control over corporate actions.

Civil lawsuits by disgruntled shareholders could also result from failure of an officer or director to exercise proper business judgment or to fulfill his fiduciary obligations to the corporation. While officers and directors can not guarantee corporate success, they must nevertheless adhere to the "business judgment rule" that they act in good faith and in the best interests of the corporation. Courts generally will not interfere with corporate decisions as long as there is a reasonable basis for the action.

Because of the liability exposure of officers and directors, corporations can provide in their charters or by-laws for indemnification to them for monetary damages they are required to pay to litigants. A corporation can also purchase insurance to cover such damages.

A controlling shareholder must avoid actions that improperly harm non-controlling shareholders. Such abuses are most likely to arise in companies with a small number of shareholders, some of whom are also officers and directors. The majority shareholder or shareholders acting together are prohibited from taking actions aimed at benefiting them at the expenses of minority shareholders or the corporation as a whole.

KEY 7

Personal liability exposure for owners of a limited liability company

---

A limited liability company, like a limited partnership, protects the owner's personal assets if the business is sued. But an L.L.C. has an advantage over a limited partnership: It doesn't have a general partner who, as we stated, has unlimited liability for business obligations.

In most cases, L.L.C. partners have no personal liability for other partners' actions. However, this immunity doesn't apply to the owners of a professional L.L.C., like law firms, accounting firms and the like. Most states still hold such "professionals" to a high standard of accountability. The state is saying, "We will let you have a monopoly in providing certain professional services, but in return you are still going to be personally liable for the business actions." Furthermore, the formation of an L.L.C. usually stems more from a desire to take advantage of various favorable tax and pension laws than from concerns about personal liability.

These professional partners have the same degree

of liability as if they were operating a professional corporation; that is, they are liable for their own actions and the actions of their employees. Most states require malpractice insurance.

In an L.L.C., all members have the right to participate in management, unless the certificate of organization provides for the hiring of one or more managers to do the job. Therefore, there is no loss of liability protection for managing the business as there could be in a limited partnership.

L.L.C. owners must take care to avoid conduct that will result in the loss of liability protection. In most instances, the type of conduct that would result in a corporate shareholder's personal liability for corporate obligations is the same that would result in an L.L.C. owner's personality: mixing together personal and business funds, paying personal debts with business funds or vice versa, using the limited liability structure to misrepresent or defraud people for personal benefit and failure to properly organize the entity.

However, as long as the L.L.C. meets its obligations there is no problem.

KEY 8

Tax aspects of doing business as a sole proprietor

An individual electing to do business as a sole proprietor must file a schedule with the Internal Revenue Service showing the firm's gross receipts and deductible expenses. He must then pay personal taxes on the net income.

Until not so long ago, the biggest tax disadvantage for sole proprietorships was a limit on deductions they could claim for fringe benefits. But changes in Federal law are being phased in to make it easier for sole proprietors to deduct retirement benefits and deferred compensation; by the early 2000's, the tax treatment for those benefits is expected to approximate that enjoyed by partnerships.

Aside from the issue of fringe benefits, the main tax consideration for a sole proprietor should be what income tax bracket he is in. If he is in a high bracket, he might want to apportion as much income from his business activities as possible to a corporation or partnership in which he has an interest, assuming that the taxes that entity will pay will be lower.

Conversely, if he is in a low bracket, he should apportion as much profit as possible to his sole proprietorship.

This approach of doing business through a variety of business forms is gaining popularity among entrepreneurs these days, both to keep taxes down and keep litigators at bay. It can get complicated, but here's a simple example. Say you own a bar and restaurant. You could put the real estate in your name, but to protect yourself from legal liability, you could form a corporation to run the business.

The corporation would then pay you rent, which would show up as income on your personal tax form. At the same time, you could depreciate the building.

The lesson: Be creative. But first, consult a good tax lawyer.

KEY 9

A partnership can be a great tax shelter

A partnership is not required to pay Federal income tax, since it is not legally a taxable "entity." But it must inform the Internal Revenue Service, on I.R.S. Form K1, how it apportions profits or losses to the partners. They, in turn, must enter those profits or losses on their personal income-tax returns.

The flow of profits or losses to the partners is known as the "pass through," and it can result in huge tax savings. A high-income individual, for example, can deduct his share of partnership losses attributable to depreciable assets.

Let's say that you expect to make $500,000 a year for the next several years in salary, bonus, interest income and stock dividends. Obviously, the state and Federal tax bite will be considerable. However, you can reduce it by investing a big chunk of money in a real-estate development partnership that is just getting started on a major building project. For the first several years, as the partnership acquires the land, subdivides it, goes through all the zoning and other regulatory riga-marole, gets the building permits and finally spends several years in actual construction, the costs will mount up. Eventually, the payoff will come, as you either sell or lease the property, but meantime, you can write off the losses on your income taxes.

If you hold onto the property, it can continue to function as a tax shelter, as you depreciate its assets. At some point, especially if you think a sale is in the works, you can form another partnership and start the whole process all over again.

You should be aware of one disadvantage of being a partner. In some years, the partnership may need to retain part of its earnings for anticipated expenses or investments. Even so, you will be taxed on your share of total earnings. Let's say earnings come to $1 million, but the partnership chooses to distribute only $500,000. If you own a 1/10 interest, you'll get a check $50,000—but owe taxes on $100,000. What's left over might buy a good used car, but not much more.

In practice, partners attempt to distribute as much of the earnings as possible after prepaying the maximum allowed expenses for the following year, relying on borrowings to finance other future costs. But sometimes dipping into the profit pool is unavoidable.

If it happens a lot, a partnership can always elect to take on "entity" status and be taxed as a corpo-ration. It does this simply by informing the I.R.S. of the change; it still remains a partnership in name and everything else. Often, partners go this route if they conclude that earnings will need to accumulate in the partnership's coffers for several years for some important business purpose. Of course, if their calculations indicate that they would end up with more money as owners of a corporation than as partners, making the switch is a no brainer.

Nothing in life is simple, however. If partners who have elected "entity status" decide later on that they would rather go back to being taxed as a partnership, they can go back to their old tax status. But they might have to wait until the I.R.S. gives its approval, and then they might have to pay whatever extra taxes the I.R.S. calculates the change requires.

KEY 10

How corporations are taxed

U nlike a partnership, a corporation is a separate tax-paying entity. It uses after-tax
earnings to pay dividends, which are then,
of course, taxed again. Salaries and bonuses paid
to the company's officers and employees are
deductible from Federal taxes, though any compensation that the Internal Revenue Service
deems "excessive" is not.

Some, but not all, corporations can avoid the
double-taxation dilemma by making a
"Subchapter S election" with the I..R.S. to funnel
all the business's profits—or losses—to shareholders in proportion to their ownership stake. In
effect, the corporation is converted, for Federal
tax-paying purposes, into a partnership. For liability purposes, the corporation still provides
investor protection. Many, but not all states, allow
parallel treatment.

In order to avail itself of Subchapter S status, a
corporation must be a domestic "stand-alone"

corporation with only one category of stock. By "stand-alone" corporation, the I.R.S. means that it cannot be part of a group, that is, it cannot have a sister company, a parent company or a subsidiary company. In addition, it can have no more than 75 shareholders, and all of them must be people, not business entities or other organizations, and all of them must be either Americans or resident aliens.

Corporations that pay taxes in the ordinary way have to be wary about building up cash hoards. Frequently, businesses, especially corporations, need to accumulate capital for expansion or other anticipated needs, and there is nothing wrong with that. Indeed, the taxing authorities assume that a certain level of accumulation is necessary for a business to function.

If that limit is exceeded, however, the corporation must be careful to have a legitimate corporate purpose for holding onto so much cash. Otherwise, a variety of penalty taxes can be imposed on the "unreasonably retained surplus." Why? Because the Government doesn't like to be deprived of tax revenue. It wants to make sure that money that isn't really needed goes to share-holders in the form of dividends, which it can tax.

Another thing starting entrepreneurs should know is that the liberal fringe benefits that corporations could once upon a time lavish on the owners are not such a great deal anymore. Some years ago, a corporation, even a corporation owned and con-trolled by a single person, was allowed to set up pension and retirement plans in more generous amounts than were sole proprietors or general partnerships. Over the years, this advantage has been scaled back, and in a few years it will prob-ably disappear. Corporations can still wring favorable tax treatment from certain fringe benefits that other business entities cannot, however. For example, the cost of some kinds of insurance, notably tax insurance for key executives, is tax deductible.

A billion here and a billion there and pretty soon it adds up to real money.

Mckinley Dirksen

KEY 11

Tax consequence as a limited liability company

The Internal Revenue Service and most states tax a limited liability company in much the same way that they tax a partnership. A limited liability company is generally regarded as a "pass through" entity if it has two or more owners; that is, the profits (or losses) flow directly to the owners and the business itself doesn't pay Federal taxes. Unfortunately, the I.R.S. and the courts haven't yet made it clear whether they will grant pass-through status to a company with a single owner.

Most states follow the I.R.S.'s lead in their treatment of limited liability companies. However, a few, such as Alaska and Florida, go their own way, taxing such businesses as corporations. And as states press their never-ending search for more tax revenues, you can never be sure exactly how they will treat limited liability companies.

KEY 12

Access to information and management participation in sole proprietorship and partnership

In a sole proprietorship or a general partnership, you have unlimited access to information. You never have to wonder how the business, or any aspect of its operations, is doing, and thus you can make informed decisions with respect to further investment of your time or capital.

In a sole proprietorship, management decisions are made by you alone. You may seek advice from consultants, but you make the decisions. Likewise, while you may delegate some decision making authority to employees, you always retain the ultimate ability to call the shots. Contrast that almost total power over events to the more passive role of a shareholder or investor in a corporation, whose access to information and whose influence on decision making are sharply circumscribed.

In making an investment of time or money, you should decide in advance how much control you wish to have over the project. If you plan to make a substantial capital investment in a real-estate development and would like to participate in management decisions affecting the project, for example, you would get a measure of control in a partnership, and total control in a sole proprietorship.

Control in a partnership is governed by general legal principles as codified in the Uniform Partnership Act or similar state statute and as modified by the terms of your partnership agreement. The Uniform Partnership Act assumes that the vote of all partners is equal. However, if there is a disparity in capital contributions of the partners, their agreement can provide for unequal voting rights proportional to their investments. After all, if partner A invested $50,000 in a real estate development and partner B invested $500,000, it is unlikely that partner B would agree to give partner A an equal vote on how the money would be spent. Partnership voting can be equal on some issues and weighted, or unequal, on others. There is no limit as to how voting can be structured in a partnership agreement, except the imagination of the individual drafting it.

On issues of day-to-day business management, a majority vote is sufficient unless the agreement provides for a higher degree of consensus. In extraordinary matters—the admission of a sixth partner, for example, or the decision to reverse course and invest money in an apartment complex instead of a shopping mall—unanimous consent is required. The point of unanimous consent is to assure that each partner retains control over the way her money is invested. Great care has to be taken in the drafting of the partnership agreement so that this control is not weakened imprudently.

Obviously, access to detailed information is necessary to make informed management decisions. A sole proprietor can only lose this access by his own incompetence, for example by ceding authority to employees or consultants or by failing to keep organized records. In a partnership, a partner also has access to the company's books and records. Partners can certainly object to unnecessary and disruptive requests for information by other partners, but they may not legally keep secrets from them. The Internal Revenue Service's requirement that each partner receive IRS Form K1 showing his proportional profit or loss, and that the partners file a joint return, further guarantees everybody's access to crucial information.

In a limited partnership, the tax-reporting requirements are the same as in an ordinary partnership, and financial information must be made available to all partners at least once a year. However, the partnership agreement is likely to restrict information by limited partners between tax returns, and for good reason. If the number of limited partners is large, responding to frequent requests for information will be expensive for the partnership and will distract it from profit making activities.

Limited partners have little direct control over day-to-day management decisions. They frequently retain the ability to discharge the general partner or managing partner for non-performance, according to a pre-determined plan. In a real-estate development partnership, for example, it is customary to give the managing general partner authority over decisions on actual construction. The contract giving the assignment to the general partner will have objective milestones in terms of expenditures of money and progress within time limits. The limited partner(s) will monitor the progress of the managing general partner frequently through the vehicle of a reserve general partner, usually a shell corporation owned and controlled by the limited partner(s). If the managing general partner fails to perform, it will be removed and the alternative general partner will step into the breach.

Frequently, limited partners can be hired to perform management functions by the general partner. Such employment guarantees at least advisory participation in management decisions and greater access to information. The pitfalls of limited partners' management participation has been discussed elsewhere but has been greatly reduced by the Revised Uniform Limited Partnership Act.

KEY 13

Ability to participate in management and access information as a corporate shareholder

The shareholders of a corporation are the corporate owners. The directors of a corporation are both corporate watchdogs for the shareholders and the group that selects the officers and sets long-range corporate policy. The officers are in charge of the corporation on a day-to-day basis and make all day-to-day decisions subject to review by the directors.

Shareholders often have little direct access to information and little voice in management's actions. However, they must approve crucial events in the life of a corporation, such as a merger with or acquisition by another company.

In a publicly held corporation, however, particularly one that trades on one of the major exchanges, the corporation is required by law to produce and publicly file quarterly financial information, including a yearly summary that describes activities of the corporation over the previous year and outlines its plans for the ensuing year. Between filing the quarterly "10Qs," as they are called, and the annual "10K," the corporation is obligated to publicly announce the occurrence of material events that effect the corporation. The concept of materiality is a relative term, of course. Much depends on the size of the corporation. The signing of a $1 million dollar contract would hardly be worth mentioning by a Fortune 100 company, for example, but could well be a huge breakthrough for a start up.

In a publicly held corporation, the assumption is that many shareholders will have made modest capital investments and will not have the time, inclination or talent to directly participate in management. Besides, their sheer numbers would make such participation unfeasible. However, shareholders can assume an indirect role by the election of directors. As a result, many corporations seek to create as diverse a board as possible, with representatives from many industries and backgrounds. They often hold staggered elections, so that the mix is ever changing. Often, each shareholder is given one vote for each share times the number of directors to be elected. This is called "cumulative voting". In this case, all directors are elected at the same time on one ballot. Each shareholder is free to cast all of her votes for one director, a technique that makes it mathematically probable that minority views will be present on the board.

In some cases, large shareholders can exercise correspondingly large influence in a corporation. Those whose holding reach a threshold percentage set by state law have the right to obtain a list of all the shareholders and solicit proxies or votes for directors, for example.

In a closely held corporation, that is, one that isn't

publicly traded, a variety of techniques exist to guarantee a shareholder's participation in management and access to information. Shareholders who wish to participate in management can frequently serve as officers. In most states, a closely held corporation has no legal obligation to appoint a Board of Directors. If it does not, the shareholders can act as the board and, as such, will have full access to all information and participate in major management decisions. Even in a closely held corporation that does have a board, techniques are available to guarantee shareholder participation in management decisions and access to crucial information. If one individual owns all the shares of stock in a corporation and seeks to attract another individual to purchase equity, he usually has to cede some of his control. If the second shareholder is asked to purchase less than a 50 percent stake, he will be a minority shareholder and can always be outvoted in a choice of directors. Therefore, before making the equity investment, the second shareholder often seeks a contractual right to choose a set percentage of directors. His resulting influence on the board will assure him of access to information and participation in management decisions. Smaller corporations sometimes will give access to information to minority shareholders and even bond holders, by contract. But such rights are strictly regulated by the contract in question and not by any tenet of general law.

Shareholders have a general common-law right to inspect and copy some corporate books and records, provided it is for a proper purpose. In some states, they must meet certain conditions, like owning a minimum number of shares, or owning shares for a minimum period of time, or both. And they can be denied to information if their request is deemed a form of harassment or if the company feels the need to protect trade secrets.

Thus, we can see that a shareholder who is not a formal or functional director or officer has limited access to information and management control. In making his investment, then, she should have confidence in the ability of the directors and officers who do have such access and control, or else should utilize one of the techniques discussed above.

KEY 14

Corporate merger and acquisitions

In a merger, one corporation takes over both the assets and the liabilities of another. In some cases, the acquiring company survives and the acquired company goes out of existence. In others, the two corporations merge into a new corporation; this is generally referred to as a consolidation. The name of the new company is often chosen to remind the public of the two prior names, especially if those names were associated with quality products or a popular image.

Discussions for a friendly merger usually begin on a management level and are quickly elevated to a board level. The board of directors of the target corporation has a fiduciary duty to recommend to the shareholders whatever it thinks is in their best interest.

A merger must be approved by the shareholders of the corporation to be acquired. A meeting of shareholders must be called, and a notice of that meeting and agenda must set forth the details of the proposed merger. The merger must be approved by whatever majority vote is stipulated by the by-laws or charter of the corporation. Shareholders of the target corporation who do not wish to participate in the merger have the right to have their shares "cashed out:" this is sometimes referred to as "dissenters' rights" or "appraisal rights." Shareholders wishing to exercise this option must notify the corporation in writing by a certain date specified by statute. The corporation is then obligated to have its value determined by appraisal and to pay off the requesting shareholders. The appraisal is supposed to be computed without taking into consideration the contemplated merger.

One reason shareholders might take this course is to avoid having to accept the shares of the acquiring company in return for theirs, a common form of payment in a merger. And if that happens, they will be required by Federal law to hold onto the new stock for one year after the acquisition, and could be subject to restrictions on its sale even after that. Some shareholders simply don't want their ability to liquidate their stock holdings limited in this way.

Frequently, a target company will reject an acquisition offer, prompting a more generous offer. But a publicly traded company can still be taken over, even if it resists all overtures. Such an acquisition, which takes place without the consent of management or the board of directors, is called a hostile takeover. It usually happens like this:

The acquiring company first purchases a position in the target company. Once it has acquired a certain percentage of the stock, it is required to file a statement with the Securities and Exchange Commission indicating the size of its stake and its intentions. Since "intentions" can change quickly, the statement is likely to claim that the purpose is as an investment only. But it can continue accumulating stock by purchases on the open market or by acquiring convertible bonds or debentures. At some point, it may make what is known as a public tender offer.

In a public tender offer, the acquiring company announces to the public that it will pay a specific price for shares in the target company provided that a quantity sufficient to give it control are offered to it by a given date. A company making a tender offer must be certain that it has the cash or credit capability to follow through.

If more than the minimum number of shares sought are tendered, the acquiring corporation has the ability to accept or reject the additional shares depending on the terms set forth in its tender offer.

All sorts of defenses are available to target companies. Golden parachutes—that is, the promise of huge payments to senior executives if the takeover bid succeeds—can be effective. The target company can also sell or spin off an asset that it knows holds particular attraction for its unwanted suitor. It can alter its by-laws to increase the percentage of its shareholders who must approve a merger.

Such defenses should be used judiciously, however; it is easy enough to put them in place but the changed corporate structure that result cannot be easily erased.

Generally, the acquiring corporation does not need shareholder approval for the acquisition unless the financial cost is inordinately high or results in huge debt.

In non-public corporations, a friendly acquisition usually presents choices to the owners of the target company. For example: Should they sell their shares, or just the corporate assets? The buyer too, must be on guard; if he buys the stock, he must take care that he is not also acquiring hidden debts or other liabilities.

KEY 15

Federal securities laws and their effect on business creation and operation

Capital needs can be an important factor in picking a business organization's format. For a business plan that requires a lot of capital, formats such as corporations or limited partnerships suggest themselves, because they allow access to capital markets. For a corporation, a sale of stock frequently provides capital. Bonds and other long-term indebtedness can also be used to finance business objectives. Sale of limited partnership interest can also produce immediate capital.

Both the Federal government and all of the state governments regulate the sale of "securities," broadly defined as an investment in a business whereby the investor reasonably expects profits primarily from the efforts of others.

If your business plan calls for a large amount of capital—say $20 million—that exceed the ability of you and your backers to supply, the only practical solution is to sell a large number of shares to the public. A corporation's first such financing is called an initial public offering, or I.P.O.; subsequent stock sales are called secondary offerings.

Before investing the time, energy and money in proceeding with an I.P.O, you should make certain that you have secured the services of a reputable underwriter (or underwriters) to handle it. It is crucial that you obtain the services of an underwriter who has a successful record in this field. An underwriter will charge a fee for its services and expect its expenses to be reimbursed, including those for so-called road shows, or presentations to brokers and institutional investors, and will seek warrants, which will give it the right to buy shares at the offering price, as part of its compensation. The Securities and Exchange Commission, however, has rules that put a cap on the underwriter's total compensation.

Try to find an underwriter capable of giving market support to the stock after it is released to the market. Frequently, a newly issued stock will perform well at first but then flounder if market support is not provided.

In preparing a prospectus, financial information must be laid out by a competent and reputable accounting firm in a format acceptable to the S.E.C. An opinion letter from a securities law firm is also advisable. PriceWaterhouseCoopers has projected that the average cost of going public for an offering of $25 million is more than $2.3 million, for example, and for an offering of $50 million, about $4.1 million.

Federal securities law provides that a prospectus will be prepared by the corporation and submitted to the S.E.C. for review. The S.E.C. doesn't comment on the wisdom of an offering; it just makes sure the prospectus discloses accurately all the information a potential investor would need in order to make a rational decision on whether to buy the shares. The agency will typically request changes, restatements or clarifications. Only when it approves the prospectus can the document be released to the public. Each purchaser of stock will receive a prospectus.

The prospectus is the principle marketing document for an I.P.O., but the underwriter can also prepare so-called "tombstone" advertisements in newspapers and magazines giving the basics of the offering—"XYZ corporation is offering so many million shares of stock at X price," and specifying that further information can be obtained in the prospectus. If you include too much detail in the tombstone ads, the S.E.C. may delay the offering.

All information in the prospectus must be factually accurate, complete and not presented in a misleading fashion. The S.E.C has clear format preferences and requires extensive discussion of all risk factors. Indeed, the reason that preparation of a prospectus costs so much is that the accountants and lawyers that write it spend endless hours analyzing it line by line to minimize the risk of a lawsuit by a disgruntled investor. In representing the company on the road show, promoters must take great care not to make any claims beyond those contained in the prospectus.

If your need for capital is more modest and your aren't ready to go public with an I.P.O., you can make a private placement under Regulation D of the Federal Securities Law. In a Regulation D offering, a private-placement memorandum must be prepared. This does not require the prior approval of the S.E.C but must be filed with the agency because by doing so you are indicating that the sole basis for the sale of stock is the information contained in the document, and you can therefore be sued only for errors or inaccuracies contained in it. In general, there must be a limitation on the number of people participating in the purchase of a private placement, and investors must usually meet specific net-worth and earning criteria that supposedly reflect a level of financial sophistication required for making the investment.

A simplified approval process exists for limited offerings of between $1 million and $5 million. After stock is sold in either a public or a private placement, Federal law requires all corporate insiders—that is, the officers and the directors—to publicly report all sales and purchases of company stock and the reason for so doing. Most well run publicly held corporations preclude the purchase or sale of stock by an insider during certain crucial time periods, notably before issuing quarterly or annual statements and before a significant public announcement.

Not only are officers and directors forbidden to trade their stock on the basis of material information not in the public domain, but the corporation might be compelled to sue its officers and directors who have so profited and recover the profit.

It is illegal for a corporate insider to tip off friends or outsiders of non-public material aspects of the company's financial existence. However, if an outsider comes upon confidential information honestly—that is, without help from an insider or without committing a criminal act to obtain it—she may trade on it.

Readers should be cautioned that this overview of securities sales touches on just some of the main features. The actual regulatory process is extremely complex and ever-changing, and business owners will need to consult professionals for guidance at every step.

They were learned not through the design of some wise legislator, but through a process of trial and error.

Friedrich Hayek,
New Studies in Philosophy,
Politics and Economics

KEY 16

State regulation of securities

Both the Federal Government and the 50 states regulate the sale of many, if not most, securities. For intrastate sales, the states have exclusive jurisdiction. An intrastate sale is one in which an entity of state Y seeks to sell its securities only to citizens of state Y. State statutes regulating the sale of securities are frequently called "blue sky laws," meaning that the authorities want them to be backed up by something of more substance than outer space.

These state laws vary widely. Some hold that if there is full compliance with Federal laws and regulations, little or nothing else is required to permit sales. Other states conduct an independent review of the business's prospectus and may limit or curtail sales of securities. Of late, many states have undertaken to establish greater uniformity among their laws. In some technical aspects, such as creating standard forms and definitions, they have succeeded. In other, more substantive, areas, considerable differences remain. It is therefore not possible in this space to discuss the various state statutes in great depth.

It can be said, however, that the states generally imitate the Federal approach. Regulations tend to be more exacting for full public sales of securities, for example, less exacting for limited sales and less exacting still for private placements.

Most states forbid the sale of securities that are not registered with their securities commission, though they make exceptions for certain kinds of securities and certain kinds of transactions.

Securities that are generally exempt from state registration include bank stock, annuities and mortgages, for the simple reason that another regulatory body is in charge of that field. Some states also exempt securities registered with the Federal Securities and Exchange Commission or that trade on one of the national stock exchanges.

Transactions that are generally exempt from state oversight include sales to a limited number of investors through corporate officers or others who receive no compensation for such sales. The purchasers of the stock in these cases are typically required to affirm in writing that they are acquiring the securities for investment purposes and not with the intent to resell.

Most states have set up streamlined procedures, such as Pennsylvania's so-called Score program, to allow small companies to issue stock in limited quantities, usually in the range $1 million to $5 million.

In addition, most states mirror federal regulation in allowing private placements on "notice filing" only, meaning that no prior approval is needed.

There are restrictions on the numbers and qualifications of the purchasers of stock in these offerings. In fact, some states have more liberal private-placement laws than the Federal government does.

States also license individuals to sell securities within their borders, and they prosecute criminal and civil fraud, and other abuses.

KEY 17

Getting funds to begin and run the business

A sole proprietor is limited in obtaining funds to begin and operate her business. Either she has saved money or she borrows it. In either case she must have enough to meet both the initial startup costs and the operating expenses until the revenues start rolling in. It's that second financial burden that can be a killer.

A lender will almost invariably require the spouse of the entrepreneur to sign the obligation. This puts at risk all jointly held assets, but if you want the money, this is what you will have to do.

Once the business starts to generate revenue, the need to borrow for existing operating expenses will diminish. But to expand the business—to hire more employees, buy or lease newer equipment, open new locations—you'll have little choice but to borrow more money.

A general partnership faces the same concerns in obtaining startup funds as the sole proprietor, but because more than one person stands behind the loan, the lender has more protection and thus is likely to be more generous. A general partnership can also raise funds by admitting new partners. Though this will diminish each current partner's stake in the business, the infusion of cash could fuel growth sufficiently to make a smaller slice of the pie worth more than it was before.

Like general partnerships, limited partnerships can raise funds from profits, capital contributions, loans or admission of new general or limited partners. Limited partnerships, which spend more than other kinds of businesses on capital costs like buying real estate or leasing equipment, generally have a clearer idea of how much money they have to raise. If they borrow funds, only the general partner is liable if the partnership assets are insufficient to pay the debt.

Corporations can generate funds from profits, loans, debt securities or the sale of shares. The startup funds for a small venture will come from the assets of the initial shareholders. If the corporation seeks to borrow funds, the lender will lend to the corporation but require the shareholders and more than likely their spouses to guarantee the debt.

Larger ventures that need to raise millions of dollars will probably have to make an initial public offering, a complex and expensive operation that requires the assistance of securities lawyers, investment bakers and accountants.

KEY 18

Doing business in another state

Any corporate entity doing business in another state must, of course, comply with its laws—including environmental, workplace safety, minimum-wage and contract laws—any and all of which can be quite different from the ones in their home state.

In most cases, they will also be subject in outside states to lawsuits for breach of contract, torts and other legal liability as well as to taxes for any business conducted.

One problem that any corporate entity can face is registering its name, for the simple reason that it might already be taken in some states.

Generally, sole proprietorships and general partnerships can do business freely in other states without filing anything. Limited liability partnerships and limited liability companies have to register, establish a registered office or designate a service company to act on their behalf and in some cases supply a statement from the home state that they they don't owe any taxes and have made all the required filings.

Corporate entities must also file to do business in another state and may have to supply a certificate of good standing. However, in many cases they can conduct certain activities in other states—like holding shareholder meetings, maintaining bank accounts, acting through independent contractors or creating as a borrower or leader a security interest in personal or real property—without registering, so long as no permanent physical presence is contemplated. You should examine each state's legal criteria for what does and what doesn't constitute such a presence.

KEY 19

Sharing profits

No matter how brilliant your strategic plan or how fat your bank account is, success for your business will prove elusive if you can't motivate your employees. The most effective means to do that, it goes without saying, is through financial rewards. These include pay, bonuses, health and pension benefits and a myriad of other perks, from free coffee to extra vacation days. But sometimes, all these together aren't enough to hold your most valued employees. In that case, you should consider offering them a share in the profits or ownership of the company.

A sole proprietor can pay her key people a percentage of earnings while retaining full ownership and 100 percent management control. Such an arrangement will diminish her income in the short term, but can do much to assure the business's long-term prosperity.

General partnerships have greater flexibility in

spreading their wealth. They can make an employee a so-called "profit partner" who gets a specified cut of the profits but no management or ownership rights. Or they can make him a full-fledged partner. He would then have to contribute capital to the partnership, but this could be financed by the firm out of his future share of profits.

Promoting a key employee to partner will of course reduce the other partners' share of income and ownership, but that won't matter if his energy and expertise help make the pie grow sufficiently to make even a smaller slice worth more. And don't forget: Today's new blood can become tomorrow's buyers of retiring partners' stakes.

A wide range of methods are available to the various corporate formats for giving employees a greater stake in the business, either through profit-sharing, ownership rights or a combination of the two. One of the most enticing, much in the news these days, is stock options, which give the recipient the right, though not the obligation, to buy a certain number of shares at a specified price over a given period, frequently five or 10 years.

Options give employees a huge incentive to work hard and get profits up, because higher profits mean a higher stock price—and thus a bigger payoff for them down the road.

Additionally, options can be a tool in retaining employees, because they often will not become vested—that is, exercisable—until a certain future date. Some options become vested over time; for example, 20 percent of the options package might be exercisable each year for five years. If the prospects for the stock are good, the likelihood that the employee will stick around is strong.

Corporations aren't taxed for issuing options so long as they follow somewhat complex regulatory requirements. But employees have to be aware that money they make in exercising them will be taxed.

Keep thy shop and thy shop will keep thee.

George Chapman, **Eastward Hoe**

KEY 20

How a joint venture works

Frequently, people talk about a joint venture as if it is a clearly defined and separate form of business organization. In reality, when you have a joint venture, you have an agreement for a very limited purpose. You might be going steady but you are not engaged and certainly, not married. You can characterize the relationship any way you wish and utilize a variety of traditional business organizations. A joint venture is not really a separate form of business organization. It is an agreement between at least two entities to cooperate on a limited scope. In its classic form, two individuals, two companies or two partnerships team up on a single project. They emphatically do not join forces on a broad spectrum of activities and, in fact, may compete with each other in some areas. But in one carefully defined sphere, they coordinate and combine their efforts and assets to reach a common goal.

A joint venture can legally exist even without a written agreement if the parties' conduct implies such an agreement. In many instances, a joint venture takes the form of an *ad hoc* partnership for a very limited purpose. For example, two construction companies may agree to a joint venture to build one specific structure. They will not cooperate on others and may, in fact, compete with each other. When the structure is finished, the joint venture is dissolved.

A joint venture can also take the form of a corporation or a limited liability company formed for the sole purpose of accomplishing a very limited strategic objective.

Please note: Whereas the partners in a partnership each has "apparent" legal authority to bind the partnership and the other partners to decisions or actions they take, the participants in a joint venture usually do not have such authority.

The need for liability protection as well as tax benefits should be taken into consideration in choosing what business form will be used to create a joint venture.

KEY 21

The desirability of a buy-sell agreement

The owners of a partnership or closely held corporation should have buy-sell agreements among themselves to place a valuation on their stakes in case they they die or want to sell out, and to assure a cooperative spirit among themselves so long as they stay active in the business.

If you own stock in a publicly held corporation that trades on an exchange, a ready market for the sale of your ownership interest exists, and you won't need a buy-sell agreement. A partnership interest or shares in a non-publicly traded corporation, however, aren't so easily marketable. The entity's by-laws may even prohibit or restrict the free transfer of such interest. In most states, the transfer of stock in a closely held corporation to outsiders is restricted either by law or by agreement of the shareholders. Often, the stockholder who wants out must first offer to sell her stake to the business itself and then to the other owners. This prevents transfer of her holding to outsiders with whom the remaining owners might be incompatible.

Setting forth the method of evaluating the ownership interest in the buy-sell agreement is critically important because otherwise the issue could go to litigation. Frequently, the agreements require the partners to write an annual appendix that calculates the value of the entire entity and of each partner's share, based on specified criteria, such as a multiple of earnings. Alternatively, a third person who is identified either by name or by the qualifications he should have can be authorized to make the evaluation. If real estate is the major asset, a neutral real-estate appraiser, business broker, accountant or commercial lawyer can be hired to make the determination or to propose a formula for calculating value.

After the death of a partner, his interest transfers immediately to surviving partners, who in turn owe the deceased partner's estate the full value of his interest. If funds are not available, liquidation of the business might be necessary. To prevent that, insurance can be purchased by the entity or by the partners to finance this obligation, such as a simple life-insurance policy covering the first partner to die. Alternatively, a security interest lien can be placed by agreement on the assets of a partnership or corporation and a formula for paying the deceased partner's heirs can be stipulated. In some instances, the surviving spouse will prefer regular, periodic payments to a lump-sum distribution, and there may be tax advantages to both parties for such an arrangement. If the entity is primarily an investment, with professional management, the heir might be acceptable as a replacement partner.

A buy-sell agreement generally stipulates that if

the creditor of one partner attempts to collect from the partnership as a whole, that partner must forfeit his interest to the others, who will pay him a portion of the value of his holding over time. If a buy-sell agreement is in place prior to the levy by the creditor, it will prevail and the creditor's sole remedy will be to garnish the proceeds paid to the withdrawing partner. If such a procedure is not in place, the creditor will frequently be at odds with the other partners and might seek to partition or dissolve the entity.

In an investment partnership, it is not uncommon for a partner to seek to withdraw his capital for personal reasons, even if he has contractually obligated himself not to do so. In such cases, litigation to establish damage for breach of contract is expensive and its outcome uncertain. A buy-sell agreement providing that upon withdrawal by a partner, he will be paid a discounted price or an agreed-upon price over a period of time can eliminate the problem.

If a shareholder in a closely held corporation dies, the buy-sell agreement can require the sale of the shares to the entity, with insurance by the entity or by its shareholders on the deceased partner used to pay the estate of the deceased shareholder. Alternately, the other shareholders can make the purchase if the corporation cannot.

In a privately held corporation, transferability of shares is limited, with restrictions varying state by state. A buy-sell agreement covering the points discussed in this chapter would do much to head off any disagreements or misunderstandings.

There are notable differences on buy-sell agreements for partnerships and corporations. In a partnership, purchase is usually required of a deceased partner's interest. Partners are frequently, but not always, reluctant to take in the estate as a partner. A corporation or the surviving shareholders might refuse to take on the obligation to purchase the shares of a deceased or withdrawing shareholder, preferring instead the first option to do so. Note: If they don't, it is quite possible that nobody will.

Everyone lives

by selling something.

R.L. Stevenson, Beggars

KEY 22

Transferability of business interests

All good things must come to an end, but some come to an end sooner than anticipated. Knowing that, you should always have an exit strategy when you enter into a business venture.

If your interest in a partnership entitles you to a stream of payments, that stream can be easily transferred to a third party. This can happen either voluntarily or, if you fail to pay your debts when they are due, involuntarily. However, the person who takes over the payments, whether friend, heir or creditor, does not become a partner and thus has no voice in management.

Another means of transferring your interest in a partnership is to sell it when you retire. In a general partnership, you will have to get the agreement of all the other partners to do this. To some extent, this problem can be dealt with by a buy-sell agreement (see Key 21).

Limited partners generally have a freer hand in transferring their interest to whomever they wish. However, some smaller limited partnerships, worried lest some notorious character take a stake in the enterprise, may reserve the right to object to the transfer to a given person. The point is, you should examine the terms of a limited partnership agreement carefully.

Ownership interest in a corporation is generally freely transferable. Indeed, restrictions on the transfer of shares in a publicly traded corporation are occur only if you have contractually agreed to give someone an option to purchase them, or have otherwise encumbered them.

A closely held corporation usually functions like a partnership; transfer of the shares can be restricted either by state statute or by prior agreement of the partners. Generally, if a shareholder wishes to sell his holding, he must first offer it to the corporation and then to each shareholder in proportion to their holdings. Also, there may be a buy-sell agreement that mandates the purchase by either the corporation or an individual shareholder of the withdrawing shareholder's stake—especially in the even of a death.

Most limited liability companies function similarly to a partnership and restrict transferability of a member's interest, though they are more likely to do so by agreement than by any legal obligation.

A sole proprietor can sell her business provided there are no restrictions related to creditors. However, if she sells only a part of her interest, she will probably end up with a partnership.

Partnerships and corporations have the advantage

of being able to bring in new blood without disrupting management or continuity. And they can arrange matters so that new owners' interest in the business will grow over time. For partnerships especially, this provides a useful vehicle for retirement; an older partner can sell his interest to an entry-level partner in stages. The portion of the sales price that represents his capital in the company is tax-free, though any money beyond that is taxable. Such a comfortable exit isn't guaranteed, of course; for it to happen, the business has to be viable and the replacement partner must be acceptable to the other partners.

KEY 23

Letting go

When it comes time for you to sell your business, potential buyers won't care a whit about the years of toil and tears you put into it. All they'll want to know is how much they can make from their investment.

An accountant can usually justify a valuation based on the assets and liabilities listed in the books, but the price you get will probably be more a function of two harder-to-measure factors: the company's earnings potential and the good will that you have built up among customers. In the end, your company is only worth what somebody is willing to pay for it. And, frankly, they are likely to pay more while you are still alive; if you have died, they will know your heirs are eager to dispose of the property and will drive a harder bargain.

Selling a business becomes a much more complicated matter in a general partnership. That is because any partner has the *de facto* power, if not always the legal right, to dissolve the partnership. That is, he may simply withdraw from the partnership, forcing its dissolution, even though that will in all likelihood mean paying monetary damages for violation of the partnership agreement.

Moreover, the withdrawing partner is entitled to her share of the business assets, less any money due as damages. So while a sole proprietor can simply wait until he wants to sell his business and then try to estimate its worth—or, better yet, hire a business broker to handle the transaction—a general partnership should probably establish a valuation method at the outset and then set an estimated price tag on the business at the end of each year.

And it would be well advised to hire an attorney to ask the hard questions and then put everything in writing. Otherwise, if the partners are getting along just fine and their business is flourishing, they are likely to put off this sensitive subject until it is too late.

For example, if a partner dies and the remaining partners wish to keep the business going, they must pay the deceased partner's heirs the value of her stake. But unless a written agreement spells out a valuation procedure and a method of payment over time, they might have to negotiate a figure and then pay a lump sum, jeopardizing cash flow.

Here is one simple way an agreement can work: Buy life insurance on each partner, naming the partnership as beneficiary, in an amount equivalent to the value of each partner's stake. Then, if and when a partner dies, pay the funds to her estate.

Sometimes, partners will decide to dissolve their partnership and cease operations altogether. In that case, their first obligation is to repay all debts to outside parties and to the partners themselves. Only then can they repay the contributions the partners have made to the business's capital. After that, whatever money is left over must be divided up according to each partner's stake.

You can imagine the disputes that might arise— over a partner's claim that he is still entitled to unpaid profits, for example, or over supposed informal loans to the company that have left no paper trails, or even over the definitions of "loan" and "capital contribution"—if a written agreement doesn't exist to clarify these matters.

Limited partnerships generally follow the same procedures as general partnerships, except that the death of a limited partner does not dissolve the partnership. Rather, the deceased's estate becomes the new owner of his stake.

In the various forms of corporate structures, unless the shareholder agrees to offer his shares to the corporation or other shareholders before selling them to an outside party, there are generally no limitations to their transfer. (See the discussion of buy-sell agreements in Key 21.)

KEY 24

The real estate investment trust: high returns, low risk

I f you plan to invest in real estate, you should consider the use of a real estate investment trust as an efficient method of aiming for the maximum return and while minimizing the risks.

A real estate investment trust, or R.E.I.T., is a unique corporate form that permits investors to pool their money for making real estate investments. Once the R.E.I.T. meets Internal Revenue Code requirements, special tax benefits become available. The R.E.I.T. itself pays little or no taxes; as in a sole proprietorship, the income and capital gains are passed through to the shareholders, who pay the taxes. This avoids the double taxation of income usually present in the corporate format, under which the company pays taxes on corporate income and the shareholders then pay taxes on dividend income.

But in a R.E.I.T., shareholders reap the benefits of a corporate structure: limited liability, central management, transferability of interest and, in the case of a publicly listed company, a ready market for their shares. The R.E.I.T. is in essence a passive conduit used to pass the income to the shareholders in a tax-efficient manner.

The R.E.I.T. gives the small investor the same ability to invest in real estate and benefit from the tax advantages that previously were only available to larger investors.

As with any investment, the potential participant in a REIT must make sure the entity was formed according to the somewhat complex rules set up by the I.R.S.

KEY 25

Which form of business organization should I use?

Now that you have read this book, you may wonder which form of business organization should you use. There is no simple answer to this question.

Generally speaking, when picking a business organization, you should consider several factors. The first, but not really the most important, is the cost of forming a given entity. Another is the extent of liability protection you will get. Another is the tax advantages and disadvantages you will end up with. Another is the ease or difficulty of raising capital. Yet another is the ease or difficulty of selling or transferring your interest to another party.

These are all criteria that you should review no matter what venture you plan. But the importance of each consideration can vary, depending on the nature of the business you start. If, for example, you enter a high-risk industry, you will obviously want to devote a lot of attention to protecting yourself against potential litigation.

Say you open a bar. Even if you follow the letter of the law, and exercise the greatest oversight imaginable, it is always possible that one of your patrons will get drunk and either injure herself or someone else—opening you to the threat of a lawsuit. With that possibility in mind, you would probably want to choose corporation as the best protection for your personal assets; it would be foolhardy to choose some other organizational structure just because you might get better tax treatment. On the other hand, you can get creative, and form a corporation with minimal assets of its own to run the bar itself and, separately, a sole proprietorship to own the real estate in which the bar is located.

If you are contemplating a real estate investment venture, you will no doubt both be looking for capital and seeking to utilize the initial losses that will occur. To accomplish those twin goals, you will have to use one of the various partnership formats described in this book.

Certainly, a sole proprietorship is by far the most common form of business enterprise in America, though of course a large number of them generate only modest dollar volume.

Professionals, like doctors, lawyers and architects, overwhelmingly prefer partnerships. If there are large numbers of partners in different geographical locations, they will probably opt for a limited liability partnership.

Family limited partnerships are frequently used as estate-planning tools, while limited liability companies are favored by those seeking the "pass through" tax advantage of a partnership and the liability protection of a corporation.

Just remember, you don't have to be stuck with any given organization form; you can switch from one to another as the need arises. You might start your entrepreneurial career as a sole proprietor, for example. As your business grows, you may decide to bring in a partner or two. As you become more successful still, you may be tempted to drift into a corporation, probably initially a Subchapter S corporation. If you succeed to the point where you need access to public capital markets then a C corporation is where you will ultimately end up. Good luck.

Please accept my resignation. I don't want to belong to any organization that will accept me as a member.

Groucho Marx

INDEX

AUTHORS

S. JAY SKLAR, J.D., has taught at Temple University's Fox School of Business and Management since 1973. He teaches a range of courses at both the graduate and undergraduate levels, dealing with the legal environment of business, corporations, entrepreneurship, uniform commercial code, the Constitution, and business. Among his recent publications are major sections of *Guide to Pennsylvania Transactions* on automotive financing, franchises, accounts receivable financing and secured transactions.

JOSEPH N. BONGIOVANNI, J.D., has taught graduate courses on commercial law and real estate for over 25 years at Temple University's Fox School of Business and Management. He is principle editor of the 15-volume set *Guide to Pennsylvania Transaction*. He has acted as a legal consultant to the business community on transactional affairs for over 20 years.